# KUDOS for Pascha Press

"Their wonderful books easily guide children through the funeral process, while helping to instill a lifelong reverence for and understanding of the importance of funerals."

—Alexandra Kathryn Mosca,
   author of *Grave Undertakings* and *Green-Wood Cemetery*

"*When My Baba Died* and *When My Yiayia Died* are welcome resources for Orthodox caregivers facing the difficult task of tenderly guiding their children through the mourning process. The author, Marjorie Kunch, writes gently and straightforwardly about what to expect at an Orthodox funeral service and the array of emotions attached to grief. Kids and adults alike will greatly benefit from these unique tools for teaching Orthodox Christians of all ages about the Church's hope-filled response to death and eternity."

—Molly Sabourin,
   author of *Close to Home: One Orthodox Mother's Quest for Patience, Peace and Perseverance*

WHEN MY BABA DIED

# When My Baba Died

## Marjorie Kunch

FOREWORD BY FATHER MILOS VESIN

*Although you feel thorns of grief at your family member's passing,
know their love will forever bloom within your heart
like an unfading rose.*

## PASCHA PRESS
Educate   Edify   Entertain

Copyright © 2015 Marjorie Kunch

All rights reserved. No part of this publication may be reproduced or transmitted in any form or by any means electronic or mechanical, including photocopy, recording, or any storage and retrieval system now known or to be invented without prior written permission from the publisher or author.

Pascha Press
http://www.paschapress.com
Toll-free telephone: 1-844-4-PASCHA
Email: mkunch@paschapress.com

This publication is designed to provide accurate information, for general purposes only, in regard to the subject matter covered. There are no warranties or representations, expressed or implied. It is sold with the understanding that the publisher and author are not engaged in rendering legal, medical, or other professional services. If legal advice or other expert assistance is required, the services of a competent professional person should be sought.

ISBN 978-0-9964045-2-5 [softcover]
ISBN 978-0-9964045-1-8 [hardcover]

Library of Congress Control Number: 2015908381

*Dedicated to all who by loving deeply, have grieved deeply.*
*Many thanks to my loving family and devoted friends, I am forever grateful.*
*Thank you to Bishop Damasceno, Father Milos, and all the priests and monastics*
*who have assisted my journey to Orthodoxy, my funeral service colleagues,*
*and to those instrumental in the production of this book by word, deed, or prayer:*
*Christopher, Everilde, Mattias; also Alexander, Faye, Irina, James,*
*Jane, Jose, Kim, Megan, Michelle, Mike, Nikki, Pam, Ray,*
*and the parishioners of Saint Archangel Michael Serbian Orthodox Church.*
*Especially my namesake, my firecracker, my lilac blossom, my Grammie.*

**ты ушёл от нас, но ты всегда в наших сердцах**

# Credits

Creative Director: Stephen Tiano
Editing: Bishop Damasceno Ribeiro and Pamela Cain Gonzalez
Images: Megan Duncan of Tricycle Motor Photography, Valparaiso, IN
Software: Fotosketcher.com

*Shot on location:*
Bocken Funeral Home
Jose Corona-Owner
7042 Kennedy Avenue
Hammond, Indiana 46323
http://www.bockenfunerals.com

Elmwood Cemetery
Michael Gozdecki-Owner
1413 169th Street
Hammond, Indiana 46324
http://www.elmwoodcaskets.com

Saint Archangel Michael Serbian Orthodox Church
Very Reverend Father Milos Vesin-Pastor
1500 186th Street
Lansing, Illinois 60438
http://www.starchangelmichael.com

Icons: Pg 14-"Entombment of Christ" Russian, circa 1900 and "Virgin Mary Iverskaya" Russian, 17th C.
Pg. 15-"Anastasis" Greek, 11th C.

Clip art used with permission by ofc.org and sourced from the public domain.

# Foreword

Dear Reader(s),

The book in your hands does not have many words, but it attempts to illustrate one of the greatest mysteries—Death and what surrounds it. We, adults—but never truly and completely mature—have our "own ways" of dealing with the matter of death; but what about children? Could we even imagine what kind of questions and images arise in their tender souls and minds? Let me, therefore, continue this Foreword with a few words addressed particularly to children:

> *When was the last time, dear children, you waited to go on vacation with your parents? Do you remember how impatiently you waited for your birthday? What about the countless days leading up to Christmas? What do vacations, birthdays, and Christmas have in common? Many children the world over, in anticipation of important events such as vacations, birthdays, and Christmas, count how many more times they have to go to sleep until the event in question.*

The Eastern Orthodox Church, in all her liturgical texts, rarely speaks to the matter of death; rather, the term used is *Falling Asleep*. This is indeed what will occur to all of us at the end of our earthly life. Does it mean that we have to wait for that moment in joyous anticipation? Certainly not. However, we must prepare ourselves. The after-life is not simply a time in which we idly enjoy the blessings promised us (provided we earned those blessings)—rather a joyful existence in which we find ourselves among Christ and His Saints, and a continual journey to perfection. Every seed, to bring forth fruit, must be buried in the ground; in other words, it must 'sleep' for a while. The very same instance occurs with us humans; in order to place a seal on the deeds we have done in our earthly life, we must *Fall Asleep* so that we are awakened for eternal life.

This book is not about eternal life, but rather how we send-off our beloved ones into eternal life. The funeral service—and all of its components—in the Eastern Orthodox Church, is mainly about two matters: prayer, and love; two matters which never die. The author of this book has wisely entitled it *When My Grandma Died*. Although my grandmother has indeed died, I continue to love and pray for her. By the faith we hold, and by the promises made by our Risen Lord, I truly look forward to the moment when we are all together; those who have fallen asleep before us, as well as those who live among us, here and now.

    Fr. Miloš M. Vesin,
    In Lansing, Illinois
    On the day of the Holy 40 Martyred Youths of Sebaste (22nd March), 2015.

# Table of Contents

PART ONE   The Visitation and Pomen   19

PART TWO   The Funeral Ceremony   25

PART THREE   The Graveside Committal Service   37

Glossary of Terms   45

One winter day, Mama and Papa shared sad news. My Baba died. Her soul was called home by God so now her body and mind no longer work. I wondered; was I bad, did I make her die somehow? I felt mad, sad, and scared. These feelings in my heart are called **grief**. Do you feel grief because your loved one died, too?

Mama said it was ok to cry and feel grief. Even Jesus wept when His friend died. Papa explained that although Baba may be gone from this life, she lives in the next. We will still pray for her when we stand in our icon corner. Nothing I did made her die. It was just time for her soul to join the **Church Triumphant**. That is what we call the people who died and live with God now. The angels rejoiced when Baba arrived at her heavenly home. Her parents awaited their reunion, even her Baba will be there!

My Baba is happy and safe with God. Together they are in a place of peace and light where tears do not exist. She is no longer sick or in pain. You may hear the priest say your loved one "fell asleep" in the Lord. It is entirely different than falling asleep at bedtime. That is just when my body rests at night and I awaken to a new day. To die is to have your soul rest and then awaken to the perpetual joy of eternal day. Imagine **Pascha**, in heaven!

Now we know a little bit about Baba's spirit, what about her body? What do we do to say goodbye to her here on earth, what do we do to help our grief? Are you curious to know what my family did next?

**PART ONE**
# The Visitation and Pomen

*Christ is risen, and the angels rejoice!*
*Christ is risen, and life reigns!*
   —Paschal homily
      St. John Chrystostom

First, the **priest** was called and he began praying for Baba to help her spirit's journey. Next, Mama and Papa met with a person called a **funeral director** to help plan her service. The **funeral** is a ceremony where we say goodbye to our loved one. Father and the funeral director will help take good care of Baba's soul and body. They will help take good care of my family. Do you think priests and funeral directors are important helpers?

Next, Mama and Papa took me to the **funeral home**. This is a building where people who died go to get ready for their ceremony. The funeral home is large so that everyone can come visit, or pay their respects, to Baba. Inside it was cozy and familiar, just like my living room at home. Families can also decide to have the visitation in their church instead of the funeral home. They can choose whichever is most comforting for them and the funeral director will make it so. I saw Baba in her **casket**. She was still, her eyes were closed, and her hands were folded on her tummy. Baba looked peaceful just as she naturally was. Some families ask the funeral director to call upon the professional services of a person called an **embalmer** to help their loved ones look like themselves again after a long illness.

A **casket** is the name of the pretty box she was in. These boxes are made of either wood or metal. I could not see Baba's feet, but I knew that they were there. Her entire body is precious and so we treat it with respect. I showed respect by being on my best behavior.

Everyone came to the funeral home to talk, cry, and share happy memories of Baba at her **visitation**. Yes, adults cry too and that is ok. What joyful memories do you have of your loved one? Everyone feels better when they talk about them.

The priest came to the funeral home and sang the memorial, or **Pomen**, prayers. He talked about Jesus and heaven. This made me feel comforted. I am sad Baba died but I do believe that I will see her again one day. Jesus said so. He promised everyone eternal life if they believe in Him.

Baba believed in the Father, the Son, and the Holy Spirit and so do I. When visiting hours ended we went home, but we will see Baba again in the morning. Want to know what happened next?

**PART TWO**
# The Funeral Ceremony

*With the saints give rest, O Christ,*
*to the soul of Thy servant,*
*where there is neither sickness,*
*nor sorrow, nor sighing,*
*but life everlasting.*
—Eastern Orthodox Memorial Service

The day after the visitation, my family gathered at church for Baba's funeral. Early morning sunlight streamed in the windows and the candlelight danced, everything was radiant.

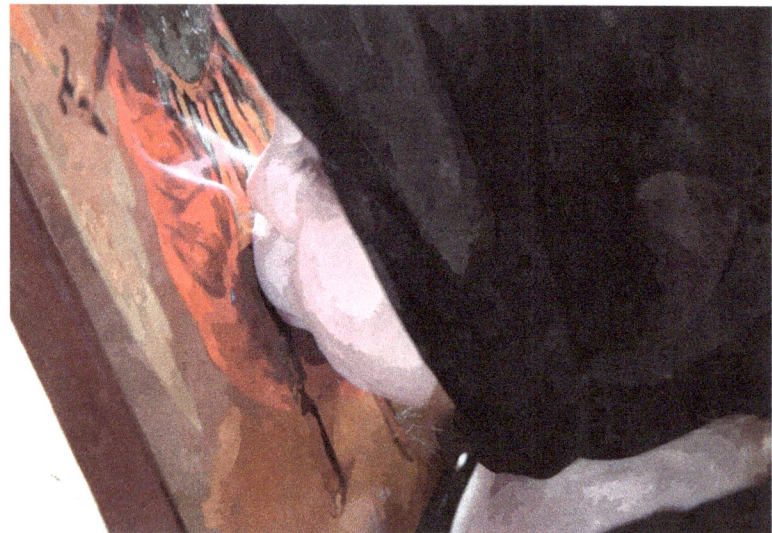

We stood in the **narthex**, or entrance, to the church and **venerated**, or kissed, the icons. Mama brought **koliva**. I held a candle. Baba got to hold something, too.

We took our places inside the church and the **Opelo** service began.

Baba's casket was opened and the priest gave her his hand cross and an icon. This showed she belonged to the Holy Orthodox Church. Father also gave her a little scroll to hold called a **Prayer of Absolution**. This prayer helped her soul be at peace.

The priest walked around Baba's casket and everybody in attendance with a **censer**. The smoke symbolizes our prayers rising to heaven. Do you think **incense** smells like Nativity, or perhaps roses? Does it make you want to sneeze?

The priest stood in the center of church and recited sacred prayers. He then went to the **ambo** and read from the Holy Gospel. Father also spoke nicely about Baba at her **eulogy**, or speech, about her life. Everyone listened carefully and let these words into their hearts. It helped our grief not feel so bad.

*Sprinkle me with hyssop and I shall be cleansed, wash me and I shall be whiter than snow.*—Psalm 51:7

Father then put a mixture of wine and oil on Baba's forehead to remind us of her baptism and bless her body. Did you know the priest anointed your body with **holy oil** when you were baptized? Every Orthodox person in the world had this anointing done to them, too.

Everyone in church walked by Baba's casket for one last kiss. I felt a little scared to lean in and kiss her while she lay inside of the casket, but Mama helped me. I was surprised that Baba felt cold, but this is because the warmth of her spirit has left her body. I silently asked God and the **Theotokos** to help me be brave. The Blessed Virgin Mary once had to kiss her Son goodbye at His funeral, too. I knew I would not see Baba again in this life except in pictures and memories so it was important I gave her that final gift. I am so glad I did.

Now we were almost done. The priest brought my family the golden cross to kiss.

Do you remember the term for when we kiss something in church?

Father blessed Baba one last time by making the sign of the cross, then her casket was closed.

The funeral director wheeled Baba's casket down the aisle. Sometimes six people are chosen from the family to help with the casket, this honor is called being a **pallbearer**. Father sang while he led everyone out of church.

Baba was then put in a **hearse,** a special shiny car built to carry caskets. We took one last trip with her and drove to the cemetery.

This line of cars traveling behind the hearse is called a **funeral procession.**

**PART THREE**

# The Graveside Committal Service

*Christ is risen, and not one dead
remains in the grave.
For Christ, being risen from the dead,
is become the first fruits of those
who have fallen asleep.
   —Paschal homily
      St. John Chrystostom*

Do you wonder what a **cemetery** is like? This is where people who died are kept. Cemeteries are restful places, like a park or garden. There are graceful trees, colorful flowers, some even have carved granite statues and bubbling water fountains. Mama said I did not have to worry about seeing dead bodies there like in the scary stories bigger kids tell. That is just make-believe.

The people who died are tucked inside their **interred** caskets, another way of saying "put away." I did see **headstones** and **plaques**, these mark where other people's loved ones are. I thought I would be afraid, but it turns out I liked visiting Baba's place in the cemetery. It's not spooky at all. Visiting someone's **grave** is a way to show love. Every time we go to the cemetery, I look around and give thanks for all of God's creation: birds, flowers, trees, and Baba.

At the cemetery, helpers moved Baba's casket from the hearse to her grave. Sometimes caskets are buried underground in a strong, protective box called a **vault**. Sometimes caskets are placed in a **crypt** at the **mausoleum**, an above ground building. Even Jesus had His earthly body placed in a **tomb** and that is why Orthodox Christians are always interred.

*"Thou art earth and to earth shalt thou return ..."*

The priest chanted more prayers. He took sand and poured a cross on the casket. This **consecrated**, or made holy, her grave. The cemetery workers came and interred Baba's casket. This is where Baba's body will stay, alongside the graves of her parents and even her Baba. Although someone has died, they will always remain a part of our family. Before everyone left, we sang "Memory Eternal" together. *Vyechnaya Pamyat!*

This concluded the funeral service, but it did not conclude our remembering, our sharing, or our love for Baba.

My family went back to church forty days after Baba's funeral and celebrated a special service called the **Panikhida**. We remember her and all of our **ancestors** at **Parastos**, **Radonitsa**, and **Slava**. These are important traditions that help us honor their memory.

As winter melts into spring, so too will our grief eventually melt into warm remembrance. My family visited Baba's grave often and when May arrived, I planted fragrant lilacs by her headstone. They were her favorite. The seasons of life, the seasons of the Orthodox Church, the seasons of nature, everything points to our Creator and His love for us.

My Baba, and all of the Orthodox faithful who have passed away, are forever remembered during **Soul Saturdays**. It makes me happy to hear the priest say her name and to hear everyone in church pray for her.

I give thanks to God for gifting us with wonderful traditions to live by and an eternal home in heaven to live for. I give thanks to God for blessing me with such lovely memories of Baba. I give thanks to God for all of the helpers.

When my Baba died, I learned about all the different ways people can help. Although I am little, even I am a helper, because I pray for Baba. Are you a helper, too?

# Glossary of Terms

**Ambo**   The raised platform from which the Gospel is read at the front of an Orthodox Church.

**Ancestor**   A person from whom one is descended. Your grandparents are an example, the grandparents of your grandparents, and so on.

**Casket**   Originally meaning a small ornamental box for holding jewels or other valuable objects, it is now the term which replaces "coffin" and is the container a deceased person is laid within.

**Cemetery**   A burial ground, a graveyard, a place set aside for the burial or interment of people who have died. Taken from the Greek word *koimeterion* meaning the "sleeping place".

**Censer**   A ceramic or metal container in which incense is burned during a religious ceremony.

**Church Triumphant**   Members of the Orthodox Church who have died and are now enjoying eternal happiness through union with God and the saints in heaven.

**Consecrate**  To declare or set someone, something, or someplace apart as belonging to God.

**Crypt**  A room or vault which is used for the burial of people who have died, also known as a tomb.

**Embalmer**  A professional man or woman who uses both art and science to prepare the deceased for their visitation.

**Eulogy**  A speech in honor of a deceased person telling of their life and all of the good things they had done.

**Funeral**  The ceremonies honoring a deceased person, held a few days after death and prior to their burial.

**Funeral Director**  A professional man or woman involved in the planning, preparation, and arrangement of funeral ceremonies. Also known as a mortician or an undertaker.

**Funeral Home**  An establishment where people who have died are prepared for funeral ceremonies and where the living gather to pay their respects. Also known as a funeral parlor, life celebration center, or mortuary.

**Funeral Procession**  A group of cars which travels behind a hearse en route to the cemetery, also called a funeral cortege. In some pious communities, it is customary for mourners to leave their cars upon entering the cemetery and walk behind the hearse to the grave.

**Grave**  A hole dug in the earth in which to bury a deceased person.

**Grief**   The normal process of reacting to a profound loss; a feeling of deep sorrow.

**Headstone**   A slab of stone set above a grave, typically engraved with the deceased's name and dates of birth and death. A memorial stone or monument.

**Hearse**   A special vehicle built to drive a casket where the funeral ceremony and burial will take place.

**Holy Oil**   The portion of olive oil that was blessed by a priest when celebrating Holy Unction for the sick and is reserved for funerals. Oftentimes it is mixed with wine, to remind us of the parable of the Good Samaritan.

**Incense**   A gum, resin, or spice which releases a sweet smell when burned upon a lit charcoal.

**Inter**   The act of putting a casket away inside of a crypt, grave, or tomb.

**Koliva**   A dish of boiled wheat mixed with honey, raisins, and other sweet dried fruit. It is brought to Orthodox funerals and memorial services for blessing and sharing with all who attend. It symbolizes the resurrection in reference to *John 12:24* and reminds us of the joyfulness and sweetness of the Heavenly Kingdom.

**Mausoleum**   A place that houses crypts or tombs, either privately for a family or a large, stately stone building constructed for many people.

**Narthex**   The porch or vestibule, the western entrance to an Orthodox Church.

**Opelo**   A Slavic word for the Orthodox funeral ceremony.

**Pallbearer**   One of six people chosen to help assist with a casket, usually the next of kin or special friends to the deceased.

**Panikhida**   A memorial service chanted for the repose of the deceased. Also called a *Parastos, Pomen,* or *Trisagion.* It consists of hymns, litanies, prayers, and Psalms.

**Parastos**   The Slavic name for an Orthodox memorial service, also known as a *Panikhida.*

**Pascha**   The great and joyous Feast of the Resurrection of our Lord, the Easter holiday.

**Plaque**   An ornamental tablet fixed to a wall, usually to mark a crypt or tomb. The equivalent of a headstone over a grave.

**Pomen**   The Serbian term for the memorial service chanted by a priest for a deceased Orthodox person, typically held during the wake or visitation at a funeral home.

**Prayer of Absolution**   Written out on a piece of paper, after singing "Memory Eternal" this prayer is read by the bishop or priest presiding over a funeral. It is then rolled up and placed in the hand of the deceased. The Prayer of Absolution is the means by which the Orthodox Church remits all of the departed's transgressions, absolves him or her from all obligations, all pledges or oaths, and sends them off into life everlasting.

**Priest**   A man specially called by God to serve His people. Ranking below a bishop but above a deacon, he has authority to administer the Holy Mysteries such as baptism, confession, marriage, and funerals.

**Radonitsa**   A Russian commemoration of Orthodox deceased observed on the second Tuesday of Pascha. On this day, after Divine Liturgy, the priest celebrates a Panikhida. He then blesses the paschal foods the faithful have brought to church. Everyone leaves to visit the graves of departed believers. At the cemetery, paschal hymns are chanted. The blessed food will then be consumed by the friends and relatives of the deceased. It is common to place an Easter egg, a symbol of Christ's coming forth from the tomb, on the graves while saying the traditional paschal greeting, "Christ is Risen!"

**Ressurection**   The most fundamental belief of the Orthodox Church, Christ died and after three days in the tomb, He arose. This Truth is celebrated every Pascha and it is what the Orthodox faithful have to look forward to after their death, arising with Christ in the never ending day of eternal joy.

**Slava**   The most significant and solemn feast day for Serbian people. On this day, families attend church services to honor their patron saint and partake of Holy Communion. It is common for the priest to then bless their house and perform a small memorial service for their deceased relatives.

**Soul Saturday**   Days set aside for commemoration of the dead within the liturgical year of the Eastern Orthodox Church. Saturday is a traditional day of prayer for the dead, because Christ's earthly body laid dead in the tomb on Saturday.

**Theotokos**   The Greek name for the Mother of our Lord and God Jesus Christ, the Ever Virgin Mary. *Theo*=God, *Tokos*=the one who gave birth to.

**Tomb**   An above ground burial chamber in which caskets are placed.

**Vault**   A container made of concrete and steel that caskets are placed within for underground burial.

**Venerate**   To regard with high respect. To respectfully bow, make the sign of the cross, and kiss a holy icon as a sign of piety and devotion. Not to be confused with worship, which belongs to God alone.

**Visitation**   Also called calling hours, viewing, or wake, a custom where family and friends come to pay respects to the deceased and show support for the surviving kin.

**V. Rev. Fr. Dr. Milos M. Vesin** is the pastor of St. Archangel Michael Church in Lansing, IL. Father Milos has authored and translated numerous books and helped produce many musical recordings. He also serves as a professor at St. Sava Theological Seminary in Libertyville, IL, teaching Church Chant, Homiletics, and Pastoral Psychology.

**Marjorie Kunch** is a mother, mortician, and Orthodox Christian who traded the snowy Midwest for the sunny Southwest. Marjorie and her husband converted to Orthodoxy on Holy Saturday 2005. She graduated Magna Cum Laude from Worsham College of Mortuary Science in 2003 and currently serves her community as a Certified Funeral Celebrant.

Blessed are they whom Thou hast chosen and taken, O Lord,
their memory is from generation to generation,
their souls shall dwell with the blessed.
Alleluia! Alleluia! Alleluia!

# ALSO AVAILABLE FROM PASCHA PRESS

### ACTIVITY WORKBOOK for When My Baba ❤ My Yiayia Died

This companion full-color workbook provides meaningful ways to help children participate in saying goodbye to an Orthodox Christian loved one. It also includes reinforcement of concepts presented such as vocabulary review and word searches, open ended questions and journaling space to help a child process their emotions, coloring pages, an icon to keep, recipes for traditional Orthodox funeral foods children can help prepare, and Bible verses to look up and discuss. Perfect for both grieving families to complete together or as a tool in the classroom to discuss the inevitable experience of death and the Orthodox response to it. Also useful for students of our multicultural society studying religions of the world or holding an interest in funeral rites and customs.

Written by a funeral director and Certified Funeral Celebrant who has served thousands of families over twelve years, this title honors Church Tradition, introduces children to Greek and Slavic cultural heritage, and evolving funerary practices.

Find this title on any retail bookseller website, ask your church bookstore to order, or contact the publisher directly:

## PASCHA PRESS
#### Educate  Edify  Entertain

www.paschapress.com
mkunch@paschapress.com
1-844-4-PASCHA

www.ingramcontent.com/pod-product-compliance
Lightning Source LLC
Chambersburg PA
CBHW042315300426
44110CB00042B/2880